Dutch Influences on English Culture, 1558-1625

BY D. W. DAVIES

FOLGER BOOKS

Published by
THE FOLGER SHAKESPEARE LIBRARY

First printing 1964
Second printing 1979

LC 79-65986

ISBN 0-918016-13-4

ISBN 0-918016-18-5 (Series)

Printed in the United States of America

IN THE days of Queen Elizabeth I of England, the Netherlands constituted roughly the region which is now Holland and Belgium and included a few border regions now belonging to France. In that age, the Netherlands was the commercial and financial center of Europe, and the English, although rapidly acquiring wealth and experience, still had much to learn about trade from the Low Countries. Most phases of the arts and learning were also vigorous and highly developed in the Netherlands, so that in almost any line of endeavor the English learned from Netherlanders.

The relations between the two countries were particularly close in Elizabethan times, but there was probably no aspect of cultural interchange which was wholly new. The two countries are relatively near neighbors, and soldiers, merchants, and others had constantly traveled between the two lands.

In early times most travelers between the countries were soldiers. The Roman legions stationed in Britain contained Batavian cohorts. When the Saxons and then the Danes invaded England, the Frisians were among the invaders; and when King Alfred was able to beat the Danes at sea, he did so by using Frisian mariners and Frisian shipbuilding methods. The tradition of using Netherlands fighting men continued; when William the Conqueror invaded England, Netherlands contingents were among his forces, and his successors on the throne employed Flemish mercenaries on numerous occasions in the eleventh and twelfth centuries. These hirelings from the Low Countries, often undisciplined and lawless, were a scourge and a nuisance in England, but a hundred and fifty years after William the Conqueror, King John (following Magna Carta)

Plate 1. The siege of Groningen (1594) by Prince Maurice and Sir Francis Vere, commanding the English contingent. The solitary soldier holding a spear immediately to the left of the group of tents (at the left of the engraving) is labeled "Colonel Vere." The formation of troops immediately to the right is the English contingent, and the formation at the extreme lower right is labeled the Scottish contingent. Engraved by Franz Hogenberg.

2

gathered an army containing the same elements and devastated the English towns and countryside. If Netherlands mercenaries were frequently a scourge and trial in England, the same could be said about English soldiery in the Netherlands. Elizabeth sent an English army to the Low Countries, but English armies had from time to time intervened in that region and the country had often been used for a battleground in the never-ending quarrels between the French and the English.

Although in the Elizabethan period religious interchanges between the countries were particularly active, this type of relationship was at least as old as the seventh and eighth centuries, when a series of English missionaries, Wilfrid, Willibrord, St. Boniface, and others, preached the gospel to the Frisians, and Netherlanders crossed the Channel to attend Bede's famous school at Yarrow. St. Ludger, a Netherlands saint, was a pupil of Alcuin at York.

Artisans made their way from the Low Countries to England in earlier times as they did in the age of Elizabeth. Some of those who came with William the Conqueror may have been weavers. Weaving is a skill found among numerous peoples on a domestic scale, but the manufacture of cloth was on a commercial basis in the Netherlands even at the time of William the Conqueror. The Frisians had much to teach the English about the cloth business. Others who came with the Conqueror may have been masons, for it was noted that whereas there were few stone buildings in England before the Conquest, there were plenty of them after it; and although brick had been used in Britain in Roman times, the small brick called Flemish tile, it was remarked, "hath been here used since the Conquest and not before."

Netherlandish workmen continued to trickle into England long after the Conquest. In 1270 Henry III proclaimed that "all workers of woolen cloth, male and female, as well of Flanders cloth as of other lands, may safely come into our realm to make cloth." In the following century Edward III also sought to lure Netherlands clothworkers into England. As one writer put it, "The king and state began now to grow sensible of the great

3

gain the Netherlands got by our English wool, in memory whereof the Duke of Burgundy not long after initiated the Order of the Golden Fleece, wherein the Fleece was ours, the Golden theirs."

Unsuspected emissaries [says Thomas Fuller in his *Church History of Britain*] were employed by our king into those countries, who wrought themselves into familiarity with such Dutchmen as were absolute masters of their trade, but not masters of themselves, as either journeymen or apprentices. These bemoaned the slavishness of these poor servants, whom their masters used rather like heathens than Christians, yea, rather like horses than men. Early up, and late in bed, and all day hard work and harder fare (a few herrings and moldy cheese) and all to enrich the churls their masters, without any profit unto themselves.

But, oh, how happy should they be if they would but come over into England, bringing their mystery with them, which would provide their welcome in all places! Here they should feed on fat beef and mutton till nothing but their fullness should stint their stomachs. . . .

Happy the yeoman's house into which one of these Dutchmen did enter, bringing industry and wealth along with them. Such who came in strangers within their doors soon after went out bridegrooms, and returned sons-in-law, having married the daughters of their landlords who first entertained them. Yea, those yeomen in whose houses they harbored soon proceeded gentlemen, gaining great estates to themselves, arms, and worship to their estates.

Although Edward III endeavored to lure Netherlanders to England, and later governments, including Elizabeth's, did the same, the result was a dislike of foreigners, especially on the part of those with whom they competed—a dislike which not infrequently over the centuries erupted in violence.

Of all the phases of the relationship, trade between the two peoples was the most pervasive and continuous. In the fourth century, grain for the Roman garrisons on the Rhine was shipped by way of the Low Countries, and there is much evidence of trade between the two countries in the Middle Ages. The chief export from England to the Netherlands for several

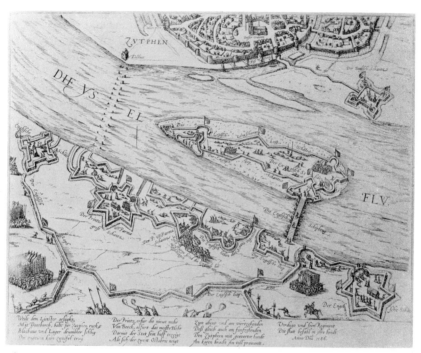

Plate 2. The siege of Zutphen by the Earl of Leicester in 1586. It was in an attempt to prevent a convoy of provisions from entering the city that Sir Philip Sidney received a mortal wound. Engraved by Franz Hogenberg.

centuries was wool. In the fourteenth century this staple was usually shipped to Bruges, but it went there by way of the present-day Netherlands, frequently passing from Orwell, near Harwich, past the port of Middelburg and down the Scheldt. Chaucer's merchant was well aware of the importance of the wool trade and the necessity of keeping the route free from pirates, for he

> wolde the sea were kept for anything
> Betwixe Middelburg and Orewelle.

The prosperity of the towns of Flanders depended on English wool. *The Libel of English Policy,* a long poem on foreign trade written about 1436, in enumerating the products of Flanders notes that:

> Fine cloth of Ypres that named is better than ours,
> Cloth of Curtrike, fine cloth of all colours,
> Much Fustian, and also Linen cloth.
> But Flemings, if yee bee not wroth,
> The great substance of your cloth at the full
> Yee wot ye make it of our English woll.

The author goes on to observe:

> For the little land of Flanders is
> But the staple to other lands ywis:
> And all that groweth in Flanders graine and seede
> May not a Moneth finde hem meate and brede.
> What hath then Flanders, bee Flemings lieffe or loth,
> But a little Mader and Flemish Cloth:
> By Drapering of our wooll in substance
> Liven her commons, this is her governance,
> Without wich they may not live at ease.

Commerce in the Age of Elizabeth. In the Elizabethan age, although there continued to be some trade in wool with the Netherlands, this export was overshadowed by the trade in cloth, which was in the hands of the Merchant Adventurers' company. The charter granted to the Merchant Adventurers in 1564 virtually conferred a trade monopoly on the company, and although they dealt predominantly in cloth, they handled other goods to a minor extent. "The Company of Merchant Adventurers," a contemporary description ran, "consisteth of a great number of wealthy and well-experimented merchants dwelling in divers great cities, maritime towns, and other parts of the realm, to wit, London, York, Norwich, Exeter, Ipswich, Newcastle, Hull, etc." At the end of the sixteenth century the company was said to number 3,500 persons, chiefly Londoners. Until 1564 the company centered its activities and trade at Antwerp, the greatest commercial city of Europe at the time. After that date the company operated in various German cities and then moved back to Antwerp, but the growing Anglo-Spanish rivalry and the turmoils of civil war in the Netherlands made that city a difficult place in which to do business. Still, until the time of the Spanish Fury (1576), when the city was sacked by mutinous Spanish troops, Antwerp remained a great market and banking center and drew Englishmen to it.

While English merchants carried on a profitable trade in the Low Countries, refugees from the Netherlands, driven to England by the religious persecution of their Spanish masters, took an increasing part in the commercial life of their adopted country. Although they settled chiefly in London, some exiles were also established at Manchester, Birmingham, Yarmouth, Ipswich, Hythe, Sandwich, Canterbury, Southampton, Maidstone, Rye, Colchester, Halstead, Dover, Harwich, Thetford, Lynn, Norwich, Boston, and Mortlake. The Netherlanders sometimes contributed to existing industries and often introduced new ones. John Leake's treatise on the cloth industry (1577) points out that because of the Low Country troubles, "the making of bays, frizados, tuftmockados, and many other things made of wool, is mightily increased in England." Leake further observes: "We ought to favor the strangers from whom we learned so great benefits, as before is declared, because we are not so good devisers as followers of others."

It is at least possible that the Netherlanders introduced cotton weaving at Manchester, and they probably began brass

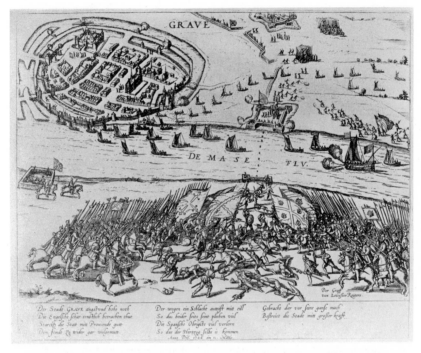

GRAVE

DE MA·SE FLV.

Der Graff
von Leicester Reuters

Der Stadt GRAVE angstvnd hohe noth
Die Engelsche schar ernstlich betrachten thut
Stärckt die Stat mit Proviande gutt
Dem feinde zu wider gar troßormüt

Der wegen ein Schlacht antrifft mit ell
So du beider seits feint plieben viel
Die Spansche Obriste viel verlorn
So das der Hertzog selbe is kommen
Anno Dni 1586 am 11 Martÿ

Gebracht dar vor seine gantze mach
Bestreict die Stadt mit großer krafft

Plate 3. A battle between English and Spanish forces outside the town of
Grave on the Maas, 1586. The Spanish were besieging Grave, the English
attempting to relieve it. The English cavalry (commanded by Sir John
Norris) is shown at the right. Leicester was not present at this particular
engagement despite the identification of his forces in the right foreground.
Engraved by Franz Hogenberg.

manufacture at Birmingham. They inaugurated silk weaving at Canterbury and the manufacture of thread at Maidstone. Cutlery was originally a specialty of Low Country workmen, and the common jackknife betrays its origin in its name, being originally a Jacques de Liège knife. Refugee lacemakers settled around Honiton, in Bedfordshire, and in Buckinghamshire; the making of lawn and cambric was also learned from the Low Countries. Dutch feltmakers had settled in England in the time of Henry VIII and their numbers greatly increased under Elizabeth. Both Netherlanders and French Huguenot refugees made felt hats in England, but the manufacture of straw hats was introduced from Gelderland. Papermaking had never been a prosperous industry in England before the religious persecutions in the Low Countries drove craftsmen across the sea, but it flourished in England after those troublous times. The same was true of dyeing, which was not a very successful craft in England prior to the coming of the Low Country refugees but which was brought to a high degree of perfection by those peoples and their descendants.

English housewives learned the art of starching from the Low Countries. The story of the introduction of this important art as given by Stow (*Annals*, 1615) runs as follows:

In the year 1564, Mistress Dinghen van den Plasse, born at Teenen in Flanders, daughter to a worshipful knight of that province, with her husband came to London for their better safeties and there professed herself a starcher, wherein she excelled, unto whom her own nation presently repaired and employed her, and paid her very liberally for her work. Some very few of the best and most curious wives of that time, observing the neatness and delicacy of the Dutch for whiteness and fine wearing of linen, made them cambric ruffs and sent them to Mistress Dinghen to starch, and after a while they made them ruffs of lawn, which was at that time a stuff most strange and wonderful, and thereupon rose a general scoff or byword that shortly they would make ruffs of a spider's web, and then they began to send their daughters and nearest kinswomen to Mistress Dinghen to learn how to starch; her usual price was at that time four or five pound to teach them to starch and twenty shillings how to seeth

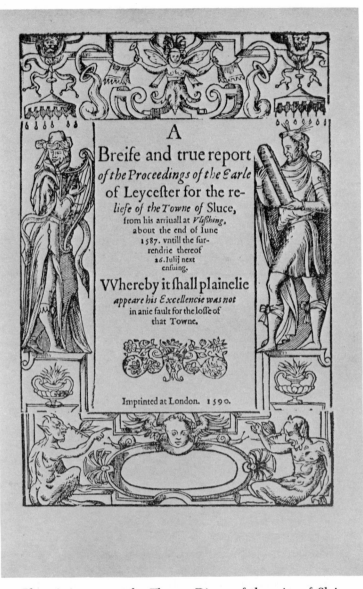

A

Breife and true report
of the Proceedings of the Earle
of Leycefter for the re-
liefe of the Towne of Sluce,
from his arriuall at *Vlißhing*,
about the end of Iune
1587. vntill the fur-
rendrie thereof
26.Iulij next
enfuing.

VVhereby it fhall plainelie
appeare his Excellencie was not
in anie fault for the loffe of
that Towne.

Imprinted at London. 1590.

Plate 4. An account by Thomas Digges of the seige of Sluis.

starch. This Mistress Dinghen was the first that ever taught starching in England.

The intrusion of the Netherlanders into English commercial life was not viewed with complacency by all Englishmen, and particularly not by native artisans. In a petition of 1616, English tradesmen noted that the foreigners were "bold of late to devise engines for working of tape, lace, ribbon, and such, wherein one man doth more amongst them than seven Englishmen can do. . . . Since the making of the last statute they are thought to be increased ten for one. Their daily flocking hither without such remedy is like to grow scarce tolerable." The English also complained that since the strangers belonged to none of the established companies of merchants and tradesmen they were subject to little regulation by their fellow craftsmen. Since many of them settled between London and Westminster, they were subject to no municipal control, either in the conduct of their business or the quality of the products they made and sold. Much of the xenophobia found expression in literature, examples of which will be given later. An antiforeign bias, or, at least, a distrust of things foreign, was also manifest in politics.

Politics. The dominant political question in England with regard to the Netherlands after 1568 was whether or not to intervene in the struggle between the rebellious provinces and their sovereign, Philip II of Spain. The revolt began in 1568 and officially ended only in 1648 with the independence of the northern provinces, the present Netherlands, and the return of the southern provinces, Belgium, to the status of a Spanish possession. Economic, religious, racial, and administrative factors had all played a part in the rebellion. In England there was a great deal of sympathy for the Netherlands and for William of Orange, who led the revolt. The English, being Protestants, felt a bond with the Calvinists, who constituted the most cohesive element among the rebels. This feeling of sympathy was strongest among the Puritans, whose adherents were to be found in high places. The growing friction with and hatred for

Spain also contributed to a fellow feeling for the Netherlanders.

Elizabeth, in the beginning, resisted any attempt to involve her in the contest. She had no sympathy for subjects rebelling against their lawful sovereign and so had no sympathy for the Netherlanders. She also genuinely loved peace and was entirely aware of the costs of war and how such expenditures could damage the economy of the kingdom. But she was also conscious of the dangers of Spanish domination of Western Europe and of the possibility that France, coming to the aid of the embattled provinces, might eventually dominate the Netherlands. The first English troops in the Low Countries, which arrived there in 1572, went as unofficial mercenaries in the service of the Dutch, but they also went with unofficial instructions from the government to see to it that French volunteers in the service of William of Orange and the provinces obtained no advantages in the Netherlands for their country. It ought to be noted that English, Irish, and Scottish mercenaries were also fighting on the side of Spain, and that some mercenaries, such as Rowland Yorke, Sir William Stanley, and Sir Roger Williams, fought on both sides.

After 1577 the danger of Spain's possessing Netherlands ports convenient for the invasion of England, and the growing influence of France in the Low Countries, caused the Queen to decide reluctantly that she must intervene. Finally, after the Prince of Orange was assassinated and after Antwerp fell to the Spanish (August, 1585) a treaty was signed by which England agreed officially to furnish troops to the Netherlands. Elizabeth sent 6,000 foot and 1,000 horse. She received in return the towns of Flushing and Brielle and the fort of Rammekens as pledges for the sums she advanced.

The first troops arrived late in 1585 and some remained in the country until well into the next century. The long years of fighting on the side of the Dutch had important consequences for the English. The mercenaries in Dutch pay, the men of Leicester's army, and the English garrisons of Brielle and Flushing constituted a large body of Englishmen who knew the Netherlands at first hand. A few of those taking part in

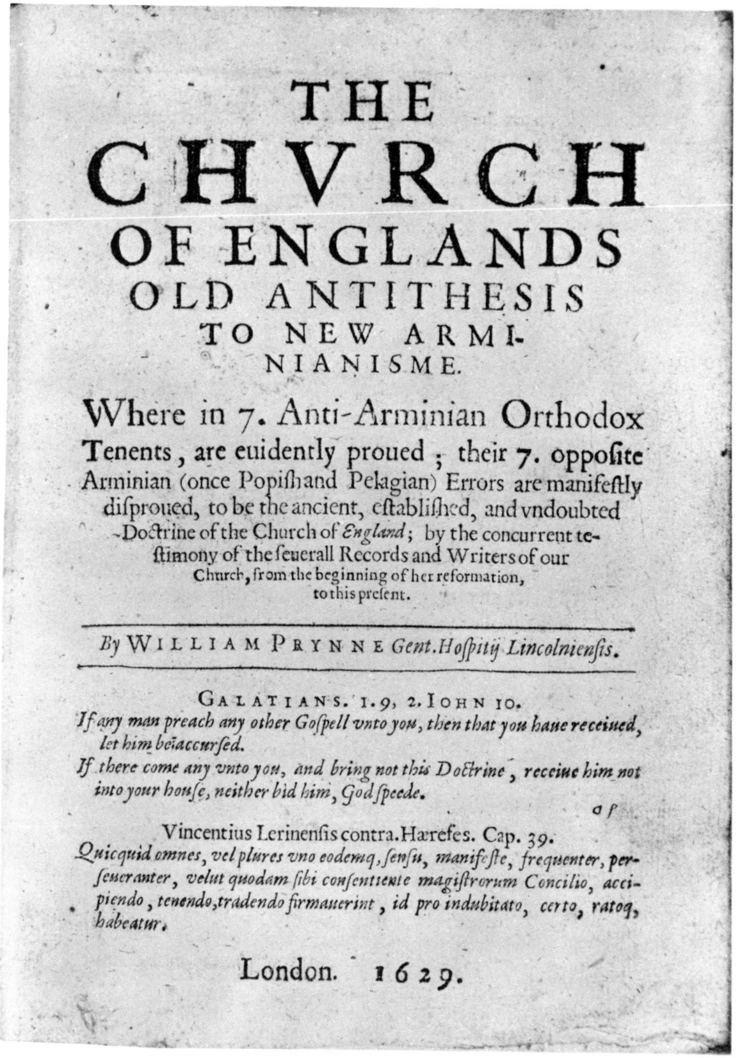

THE
CHVRCH
OF ENGLANDS
OLD ANTITHESIS
TO NEW ARMI-
NIANISME.

Where in 7. Anti-Arminian Orthodox
Tenents, are euidently proued ; their 7. oppofite
Arminian (once Popifh and Pelagian) Errors are manifeftly
difproued, to be the ancient, eftablifhed, and vndoubted
Doctrine of the Church of *England*; by the concurrent te-
ftimony of the feuerall Records and Writers of our
Church, from the beginning of her reformation,
to this prefent.

By WILLIAM PRYNNE *Gent. Hofpitÿ Lincolnienfis.*

GALATIANS. 1.9, 2. IOHN 10.
If any man preach any other Gofpell vnto you, then that you haue receiued,
let him beiaccurfed.
If there come any vnto you, and bring not this Doctrine, receiue him not
into your houfe, neither bid him, God fpeede.

Vincentius Lerinenfis contra. Hærefes. Cap. 39.
Quicquid omnes, vel plures vno eodemq, fenfu, manifefte, frequenter, per-
feueranter, velut quodam fibi confentiente magiftrorum Concilio, acci-
piendo, tenendo, tradendo firmauerint, id pro indubitato, certo, ratoq,
habeatur.

London. 1629.

Plate 5. A typical attack on the Arminians, William Prynne's *The Church of England's Old Antithesis to New Arminianism* (1629).

the fighting were the Earl of Leicester, Sir Philip Sidney, Sir Fulke Greville, Sir Roger Williams, Sir Humphrey Gilbert, Ben Jonson, George Gascoigne, and three members of the Sherley family.

The English army that went into the Netherlands was an antiquated force with the most rudimentary organization, outmoded weapons, and incompetent leaders. The Netherlands and subsequently the French wars hardened and hammered the English troops into a first-class fighting force. The intervention in the Netherlands led to intervention on the side of Henry IV in France, and to some extent the English policy of maintaining a balance of power in Europe was formed during these years. The Netherlands wars gave impetus to the publication in England of many books on the art of war. The conflict left its impression on English letters, English speech, and English seafaring, and the drainage of the Fens got fresh impetus from soldiers who observed Low Country drainage methods.

Religion. During the reign of Elizabeth, thousands of Netherlands Protestants fled to England to avoid religious persecution by the Spanish authorities. Before the civil wars ended an estimated 100,000 Netherlanders had fled their homes, the majority taking refuge in England. It is said that during the reign five-sixths of the foreigners in England were Dutch, and although this figure included Germans, nevertheless reports agree that the number of Netherlanders was remarkably large.

The great majority of those fleeing to England were Calvinists. The dominant system of religious thought in England at this time, both among those who conformed to the Established Church and those who dissented from it, was also Calvinism, so that it cannot be said that the Dutch Calvinists brought anything new to the country. The refugee Calvinists simply reinforced and perhaps invigorated what was already there.

In addition to Calvinists, minor sects were also represented among the refugees. Of the lesser groups the Anabaptists were the most numerous, feared, and misunderstood. The sect was originally German rather than Dutch, but it gained thousands of adherents in the Low Countries. Anabaptists were found in England and persecuted before the reign of Elizabeth, and the persecution continued into her reign. According to Camden, a royal proclamation of 1561 ordered "Anabaptists and suchlike heretics" to leave the realm within twenty days, but in spite of the order many Anabaptists continued in the country. In 1575 an Anabaptist congregation at Aldgate was discovered and broken up, two of its members being burned at Smithfield "in great horror with roaring and crying." In 1589 there were said to be several congregations in London, and the sect continued to exist, if not to flourish, in England.

One of the most remarkable facts about the Anabaptists was the influence they exerted on others: both the Baptists and Quakers, for example, owe some of their ideas to the Anabaptists. All Baptists have the Netherlands in their origin, but it is the General Baptists, as distinguished from the Particular Baptists, who were influenced by the Anabaptists. The General Baptists had their beginning in a group of English Brownists who fled to the Netherlands. At one point they worshipped in Amsterdam in the same building with the Anabaptists. Some of them became Anabaptists, while others returned to England and eventually became the General Baptists; but although these latter had refused to become Anabaptists they were powerfully influenced by the sect and by their former companions who had become Anabaptists. The Particular Baptists also have the Netherlands in their background, for they stem from an independent congregation organized at Southwark by Henry Jacob, a former Puritan refugee at Leyden. The Quakers were not organized until the mid-seventeenth century, but their historian, Robert Barclay, was convinced that the founder of the sect, George Fox, had been influenced, perhaps unconsciously, by Anabaptist doctrine.

Another Netherlandish sect, a most eccentric one, which was transplanted to England, was the Family of Love, or the Familists. The acknowledged founder of the sect was Hendrik

Plate 6. Orlando di Lasso, from Jean Jacques Boissard, *Icones . . .
virorum illustrium* (1597).

Niclaes, and although the group was first formed in Emden it spread throughout the Netherlands. There is evidence that, like the Mormons, the Familists practiced polygamy, and, like the Mormons, they had, at least in theory, a tight hierarchical organization. The Familist doctrine has been characterized as a mystic pantheism, and there was also a strong antinomian tendency. Niclaes taught that nothing about the body was unclean, and the "naked runners" reported on the Continent as being Anabaptists were probably members of the Family of Love. Forced to leave Emden in 1560, Niclaes went first to the Netherlands, then to England, and finally to Cologne.

In England, the Familists were first established among the refugee Dutch communities, but the sect soon had adherents among the natives also. The leader in England was Christopher Vitel, a native of Delft, who resided at Colchester and at Southwark. In 1574 the government proceeded against the Familists and the sect appealed to Parliament. The appeal, which was published in 1575, was entitled *An Apology for the Service of Love and the People That Own It*; and it was probably in the same year that Christopher Vitel translated and published one of the principal works of his master, Niclaes, with the title *Introductio; An Introduction to the Understanding of the Glass of Righteousness, Set Forth by HN*. Elizabeth issued a proclamation against the sect in 1580, and the Familists also incurred the wrath of James I, who mistakenly held them responsible for the rise of Puritanism. The group survived in England until the eighteenth century. It is worth noting that some writers have seen a striking parallel between Bunyan's *Pilgrim's Progress* and a biography of Niclaes published in 1550 entitled *Mirabilia opera Dei: Certain Wonderful Works of God, Which Happened to HN*.

Of all the religious doctrines developed in the Netherlands, one of the most influential and interesting was Arminianism. The cardinal characteristic of the Arminians, or Remonstrants, as they came to be called, was their rejection of the Calvinistic doctrine of predestination. Since England was largely Calvinist, the Remonstrants were at first viewed with disfavor in England, but the rejection of predestination led the Remonstrants into other assertions which Anglicans could only applaud. For example, the Remonstrants, fearful of their fate at the hands of their Calvinist fellow Christians, argued that the civil authorities ought to be the court of last resort in religious disputes. When Vossius, a noted Dutch theologian, on his visit to England not only reiterated the Remonstrant position of the supremacy of the civil magistrate in religious matters but advanced from that position to argue the divine right of kings, the Remonstrants grew in favor with the Anglicans. Conversely they grew in disfavor with the nonconformists and "Arminian" became with the Puritans and other dissenters a term of opprobrium and abuse.

Not only were there religious refugees from the Netherlands in England, but English religious refugees were never so numerous in the Netherlands as they were in this period. Americans know that Robinson and his Puritans, the "Mayflower" group, began to migrate to Amsterdam in 1607 and that they were settled in Leyden in 1609, but this group was only one of several dissenting communities in the Low Countries. Another Puritan congregation settled at Middelburg, and Thomas Cartwright, a famous Puritan, was one of its pastors. The Brownists led by Robert Browne also settled at Middelburg. Browne, a former Church of England clergyman, had lived at Norwich, which thronged with Netherlanders, many of them Anabaptists. Browne was soon preaching Anabaptist doctrine, and he and his group fled in fear of persecution to the Netherlands in 1581.

An interesting consequence of the presence in the country of the dissenting groups was that the Low Countries became the publishing center for nonconformist literature. Not only were the writings of English exiles in the Netherlands published, but also manuscripts were sent from England to be published at Dort, Middelburg, and Amsterdam.

Just as the North Netherlands became a haven for dissenting English Protestants, so the South Netherlands became a place of refuge for English Catholics. Fearful that the supply of Eng-

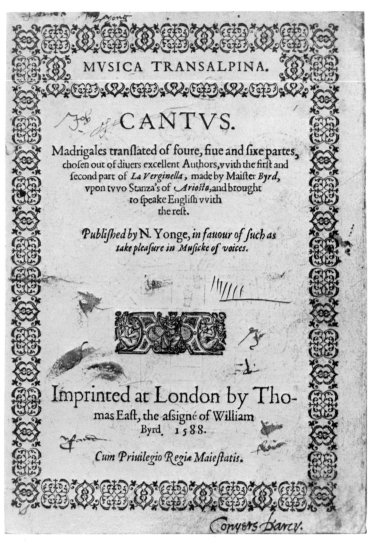

Plate 7. The title page of Nicholas Yonge's *Musica Transalpina* (1588).

lish-speaking priests would be insufficient, William, Cardinal Allen, a leader of the Catholic exiles, with the collaboration of other divines founded a seminary for English priests at Douai in 1568, and missionaries from that college returned to labor in the Catholic cause in England. Because of trouble caused by the wars in the Netherlands, the English college was removed to Reims in 1578. The English Catholic students returned to Douai in 1593 and the South Netherlands continued to be a refuge for English Catholics. As the North Netherlands became the publishing center for Protestant dissenting literature, so the presses of Douai, Louvain, and Antwerp supplied England with contraband Roman Catholic books.

Architecture. During this period the Netherlands exerted a remarkable influence on English arts and crafts. At the beginning of the reign of Henry VIII the dominant foreign influence in England had been the Italian Renaissance, but Henry's break with the Roman Catholic church resulted in England's becoming not only anti-Roman Catholic but to a large extent anti-Italian as well. In architecture, sculpture, painting, and even in personal manners, an Italianate style became a thing of scorn. The way was thus opened for Netherlandish influence, and in architecture it was a considerable one. The effect of the Italian Renaissance had been the same in the Low Countries as in England; that is, influence was evident in the decoration of buildings rather than in their basic structure. In the Low Countries the chief influence was not exerted by the Renaissance architects, properly speaking, but by the successors to that great age, the mannerists of the first half of the sixteenth century. The pinnacles, urns, pilasters, scrolls, caryatid pilasters, and consoles with which Low Country builders covered their façades are copies of the decorative devices of the mannerists. Also, much of the form and decoration of that most typical Netherlandish architectural feature, the gable end, originated in Venice, where it can be seen on the façades of churches, on church wainscotting, and on the bratticing of choir stalls. The most prevalent Low Country decorative device was strapwork, stonework imitation of the curves and flourishes which can be formed with leather bands. Sometimes the straps are simply outlined in stone, but usually they are three-dimensional, raised and interlaced against the background. When the way was opened for a Netherlands architectural influence in England, these decorative devices, classic designs at third and fourth hand, were transferred to English buildings. The Low Country influence came to England in the usual ways, through refugees, through English travelers in the Netherlands, and through books. Among the refugees fleeing from persecution by Alva were joiners, carvers, and master masons; and while the great majority of building trade mechanics were English, the Netherlanders exercised an influence out of proportion to their numbers.

In that age, master workmen executed their own designs, and finish work in Elizabethan buildings, such as carved stair rails, newel posts, wainscotting, doorframes and window frames, frequently exhibits typically Netherlandish designs. When Henry VIII began construction of Nonsuch Palace, he "invited thither at the royal cost of the most excellent artificers, architects, sculptors, and statuaries of different nations, Italians, Frenchmen, Hollanders, and native Englishmen." Actually, although other nationalities are mentioned here, the great majority of mechanics and artificers arriving in England at this time were Netherlanders or Germans, and usually the former. At Hatfield, a Dutch joiner named Janivere was responsible for most of the wainscotting and chimney pieces; the wood turning was done by one Hooker, probably also a Netherlander; and the designer of one of the fireplaces was Maximilian Colt, a well-known Low Country sculptor.

Sometimes Englishmen who had lived or traveled in the Netherlands deliberately imported Netherlandish architecture, an example being Sir Thomas Gresham, long a resident at Antwerp. The London Royal Exchange, which he had built in the years 1566–1571, was probably designed by Henri van Pas, or Paschen, of Antwerp. Many features of the structure were in imitation of the Bourse at Antwerp, and the clock tower resembled the clock tower on a Netherlands town hall. The building was of brick, the court was paved with brick brought from the Netherlands, and many of the workmen employed were Netherlanders.

A more potent influence on architecture than either Low Country artisans or English travelers was Netherlandish books. English books of the Elizabethan period are usually without either illustration or decoration, but Netherlands books were often illustrated and frequently had engraved title pages and ornaments which incorporated the triumphal arches, pilasters, cartouches, caryatids, and strapwork which have been mentioned. The numerous maps published in the Netherlands at the time also were decorated with dolphins, scrolls, and mythological figures. An English workman did not have to be able to read the books in order to copy the designs he found in them. As a result of the demand for designs, pattern books also were published—volumes whose sole purpose was to provide decorative devices for whoever needed them.

While some of these pattern books were French, Italian, or German, most of them were compiled by Netherlanders and were issued in the Netherlands. The designs they portrayed eventually appeared on English façades, ceilings, paneling, and fireplaces. Aside from this influence on decoration, the only notable structural influence Dutch architecture seems to have had in England was in the placement of the gable end of a building toward the street or the front of the structure, and the concealment or modification of its triangular shape by a curved or stepped façade.

Painting. While the influence of the Low Countries on architecture largely affected only the decoration of structures, in painting the Netherlanders simply overwhelmed the native artists and painting in England became a Netherlandish art. It has been asserted that an exhibition of paintings executed during the first seventy years of the century would contain scarcely a work by a native artist. After 1570 some English artists became prominent, but the art or business of portraiture remained

Plate 8. Jan van der Noot's emblem book, a Dutch edition printed in England in 1568.

in Netherlandish hands. In the Netherlands and Italy at this time portraits were produced in factories, large studios presided over by a man of talent assisted by many men of lesser ability, and the Netherlanders evidently transferred this system of producing portraits to England. That many English portraits originated in such factories is indicated by the appearance of the same techniques, the same arrangements of hands and feet, the same or similar cushions, curtains, and floor coverings in portrait after portrait. The portrait factories were directed by outstanding Netherlands artists whose work is well known, and staffed by numerous lesser Netherlanders, whose names and occupation appear in church and civil records.

Among the prominent painters was Hans Eworth, or Ewoutsz, of Antwerp, who came to England in 1543 and was still working in 1574. For a long time his monogram HE was thought to be that of Lucas de Heere, another well-known Netherlands painter who lived and worked in England. Two Netherlandish painters at the court of Queen Elizabeth about whom a great deal is known are Marcus Geeraerts the elder and Marcus the younger, father and son. Marcus the younger married a sister of John de Critz, a Netherlands artist working in England who was more widely known than Marcus himself. The painter Paul van Somer was more widely known than either of them, and he was succeeded in royal favor by another Netherlander, Daniel van Mytens.

The men who have been mentioned were artists of the first rank. There were plenty of Low Country artists in England of second and third rank, and one of them, Martin Droeshout, ought to be at least noted. The Droeshout family was originally from Brabant, and two brothers, Michael and Martin Droeshout, were living in England in the early seventeenth century. Martin had a son, also called Martin, who engraved the portrait for the first folio edition of Shakespeare's works.

Engraving. About 1560 so many engravers were living in Antwerp that the city had a virtual monopoly of the art. The numerous maps and atlases produced in the Netherlands gave employment to large numbers of engravers, and book production gave work to others. Many of these artists and craftsmen migrated to England, and probably the earliest line engraver working in England, Thomas Geminus, had come from Flanders. One of the most famous of Netherlands map engravers, Jodocus Hondius, worked for a time in England, as did two other well-known engravers who had executed maps, Franz and Remigius Hogenberg of Malines. Another well-known Low Country artist, Theodor de Bry, whose illustrations to his collections of voyages are widely known, also worked in England for a time. The men mentioned are but a few of a host of Low Country men who engraved views, portraits, and maps in England.

Sculpture. One of the most noted Netherlands sculptors to settle in England was Gerard Janson, or Geraert Janssen, the elder, of Amsterdam. More than fifty monuments in England have been attributed to him, and he also executed the portrait bust of Shakespeare at Stratford-on-Avon after 1616. Two sculptors from Arras, Joseph Hollemans and Maximilian Colt, also achieved fine reputations in England, and the Cure, or Cuer, family were men of importance for three generations. William Cure, or Cuer, a stone carver, was brought to England when Henry VIII was building Nonsuch. His son, Cornelius Cure, was master mason to Queen Elizabeth, and his grandson, William Cure, master mason to James I. Both Cornelius and William executed important monuments. As in the case of painters and engravers, there were numerous Low Country sculptors whose work can be identified only sketchily, if at all. It is known, for example, that Bernard Jansen, or Janssen, was a stone mason and tomb maker employed at Audley End, and a certain Giles de Witt, marbler, was at work at Cobham in 1594. In the lugubrious art of designing tombs, the influence of Flemish stone carvers and master masons is distinctive. Well into the second half of the sixteenth century the usual tomb was the traditional medieval stone table surmounted by a recumbent effigy, but the Flemings introduced the architectural tomb, characterized by a canopy supported on pillars and decorated with heraldic sculpture.

Music. The Netherlands influenced English music both directly and indirectly, since the Netherlanders influenced Italian music, which in turn influenced the art in England. In the second quarter of the fifteenth century, largely through the work of musicians in the southern provinces, a distinctive Low Country school of music emerged. Soon the courts of Germany, Spain, France, and Italy were endeavoring to attract Netherlands musicians, and for 150 years, roughly the period 1450–1600, the Netherlanders continued to enjoy a dominant position in music. Henry VIII was a lover of music and a fair composer. Like other princes he recognized the richness of Netherlands music, and a number of musicians at the English court were Low Country men. Indeed, by the end of the fifteenth century the Flemish polyphonic style was so familiar in England that it was probably considered English rather than foreign. The great opportunities for the Netherlands polyphonic style were in masses and motets, but the Reformation denied this means of expression to English musicians. The technique and musicianship which Englishmen had learned from their Netherlands colleagues emerged in the age of Eizabeth in the so-called "great" service of the Anglican church.

Some of the Low Country migrants to Italy are quite well known. Adrian Willaert, born in Flanders about 1480, was the renowned organist at St. Mark's in Venice and the founder of the Venetian school of music. He was followed by Jacques Arcadelt, probably born at Liège about 1514, who went to Italy in 1538, and by Philippe Verdelot, born in Flanders but a long-time resident in Italy. Two other well-known Netherlandish musicians who visited Italy were Nicolas Gombert and Clemens non Papa (Jacob Clemens). Many people who know the music of Orlando di Lasso fail to realize that he was born Roland de Lattre at Mons in 1532. Lasso's famous contemporary Philippe de Monte was born at Malines, migrated to Italy, and ended his days in the service of the Hapsburgs at Vienna. To these great Netherlandish names in music history may be added two others of renown, the Fleming Thomas Crecquillon, and Cyprien de Rore, who was born at Malines but lived in Italy for many years.

All the great Netherlanders in Italy composed madrigals. The first leader of the Flemish madrigalists was Willaert. Lasso and Philippe de Monte also wrote madrigals, and the most famous Italian madrigal of all, "Il bianco e dolce cigno," was composed by Arcadelt. The singing and playing of madrigals became a favorite diversion of the Elizabethans, who imported them from Italy before such music was published in England. The first collection of madrigals to appear in England, *Musica Transalpina*, was brought out by Nicholas Yonge in 1588, about fifty years after such songs achieved popularity in Italy. Yonge, in the dedication to *Musica Transalpina*, speaks of entertaining guests in his house by "furnishing them with books of that kind yearly sent to me out of Italy and other places." Thus it was by way of Italy and the madrigals that Netherlanders exerted an influence on English secular music, an influence probably greater than that exerted by Low Country musicians migrating to England.

Tapestry, Stained Glass, and Glassware. In the minor arts the Netherlanders also made a contribution and in tapestry weaving a large one. Although wallpaper had been used as early as the reign of Henry VIII, and paneling had a great vogue in Tudor times, the demand for tapestries persisted. England's customary source for tapestry was the Low Countries, and, even after tapestries were woven in England, the bulk and the best of them continued to come from there. When it was decided to commemorate that great national event, "The Defeat of the Spanish Armada," in tapestry, the panels were executed abroad. Admiral Lord Howard conferred on the designs with Henry Cornelius van Vroom, a painter of Haarlem skilled in the pre-

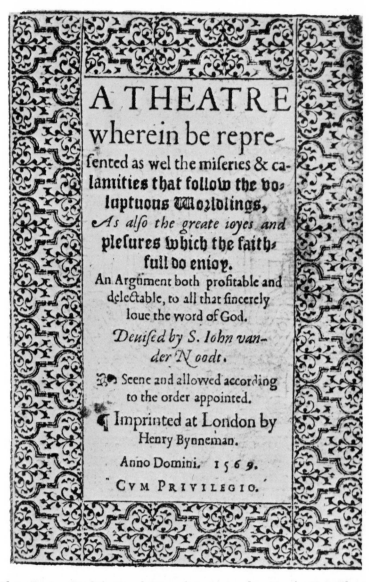

A THEATRE

wherein be repre-
sented as wel the miseries & ca-
lamities that follow the voluptuous Worldlings,

As also the greate ioyes and
plesures which the faith-
full do enioy.

An Argument both profitable and
delectable, to all that sincerely
loue the word of God.

Deuised by S. Iohn van-
der Noodt.

Scene and allowed according
to the order appointed.

¶ Imprinted at London by
Henry Bynneman.

Anno Domini. 1 5 6 9.

CVM PRIVILEGIO.

Plate 9. An English translation of Jan van der Noot's *Het Theatre*,
printed in 1569.

sentation of marine battles, and the execution was entrusted to François Spierincx, master tapestry weaver of Antwerp and Delft.

About the middle of the sixteenth century a number of tapestry weavers were at work in England. William Sheldon, an English country gentleman who opened a tapestry atelier, sent one Richard Hyckes, or Hickes, to the Low Countries to learn the art. The best known of the English ateliers was that established at Mortlake in the reign of James I. Sir Francis Crane had proposed that a factory be established of sufficient size and excellence to handle any commission. King James became interested in the proposal in 1619 and offered through his agents in the Low Countries to bring over a sufficient number of capable workmen. The Netherlanders were brought over in such secrecy that the factory was in operation before the Netherlandish authorities were aware of the departure of some of their best workmen. The following year, 1620, the secretary to the Netherlands embassy reported with grave concern to his government that the enterprise of King James at Mortlake was a serious threat to the Dutch tapestry industry.

Glass was made in small quantities in England in the Middle Ages and perhaps in Roman times, but a great expansion of the industry occurred under Elizabeth. English glass and glassware manufacture owed much to the Netherlands, for although glassware was largely a Venetian art, it was mainly transmitted through the Netherlands, and sheet glass was introduced to a large extent from the Netherlands as well as from France. At the beginning of the sixteenth century, the rich lived in houses with windows of horn or selenite and drank from glasses imported from Italy, while poorer folk drank from vessels of horn, wood, or leather. By the middle of the reign of Elizabeth, glass from Normandy, Burgundy, and Flanders was used in the windows of great houses, and glassware was quite common among the well-to-do. The great change had come about largely because of the difficult conditions in the Venetian glass factories in the years immediately before 1550. Despite the enormous demand for glass in Western Europe, the Venetian entrepreneurs deliberately kept production low. They persisted in this restrictive policy even though glassmakers in Venice were out of work. The unemployed workmen were eager to go elsewhere, but the laws of Venice forbade the workmen to leave Venetian territory under pain of heavy punishment. In spite of the prohibition, a number of Venetian glassmakers migrated to the Netherlands about 1539, and the art became firmly established in Flanders. Ten years later, other Venetian glassmakers went to England for a stay of eight or nine months, with the result that glass factories were also established in that country. In the subsequent history of English glassmaking, the native industry was overshadowed by the activity of Low Country workmen and entrepreneurs who expanded to England.

The Netherlandish expansion may be thought to begin with John Carré of Arras and Antwerp, who in 1567 obtained a license to manufacture glass in England. For more than fifty years Carré and those who succeeded him staffed their establishments largely with Venetians or men of Venetian descent who had been employed in the glass factories of the Netherlands.

A great deal of the stained glass in England was also made by Netherlanders, and in such lesser arts as furniture design and jewelry making the Netherlanders were also influential.

Printing and Publishing. Books printed in the Low Countries influenced architecture, design, music, religion, and other phases of English life. In addition Netherlands printers influenced the trade of printing itself. Among the refugees were many printers and bookbinders. The lot of these men was especially difficult, because printing and publishing were tightly controlled and restricted to members of the Stationers' Company, and the foreigners, not being members, had no right to print and publish books. Still, the competence and skill of the foreigners, in general superior to that of the native printers, was bound to be recognized and employed. Sometimes foreigners worked for wages in the shops of members of the Stationers' Company; sometimes they were given the status of brothers of

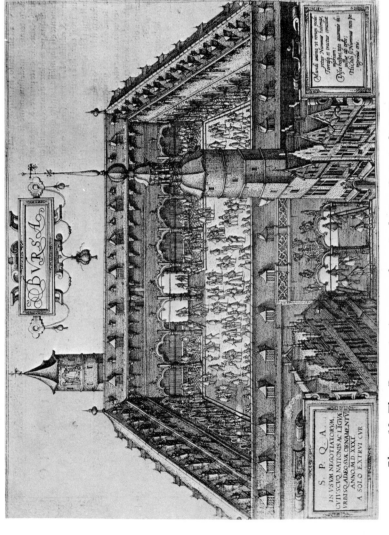

Plate 10. The Bourse in Antwerp, from Lodovico Guicciardini, *Descrittione . . . di tutti di Paesi Bassi* (1591).

the Company. As brothers they might maintain shops, but they could not bind apprentices, nor could they print books except as work done for members of the Company. With such limited opportunities, the aliens nevertheless made their competition felt, as is apparent from "A Petition of the Poor Men of the Stationers' Company for Relief," dated 1578, in which the petitioners prayed that the Court of the Stationers' Company would decree that "Frenchmen and strangers, being denizens, may not have excessive number of apprentices." The Court of the Company replied that no strangers had apprentices, although apprentices bound to members of the Company sometimes were set to work in the shops of aliens; and the Court then reminded the petitioners that there was nothing to prevent members of other companies, goldsmiths, or mercers, for example, from setting out their apprentices to the foreign workmen and thus learning the whole art of printing. Some Huguenots and Netherlanders did become members of the Company, but for the great majority of refugee printers the situation was difficult.

The printing of English books in the Netherlands affected English printing and publishing also, since in time the devices for surreptitious publishing in the Low Countries became perfectly known to English booksellers, who thereby became less dependent on English printers. English books were printed at Antwerp to a greater or less extent throughout the sixteenth century. In the first third of the century, although a few secular books were issued, the bulk of the product consisted of missals, processionals, manuals, psalters, hymnals, breviaries, and horae intended for the English market. Also, several editions of Tyndale's New Testament were issued at Antwerp (1534–1538). The Coverdale Bible was perhaps printed at Antwerp, as was the composite version known as "Matthew's Bible" (1537). In the brief period 1534–1538, books intended for English Protestants were issued. This was followed by a period of meager English printing, but in the last third of the century many English books were issued, not only at Antwerp but in other Netherlands cities. English nonconformists published their works at Middelburg, Dort, Leyden, Amsterdam, and elsewhere, and English Catholics published at Douai, Louvain, and Antwerp. From 1564 to 1569 Diest and Laet at Antwerp and Bogard and Foulder at Louvain between them printed forty English books by such English Catholic authors as Harding, Rastell, Martiall, Stapleton, Allen, and Sanders. At Douai, English printing was probably more extensive than it was at either Louvain or Antwerp. While the first Roman Catholic version of the New Testament was printed at Reims in 1582, the first English version of the Old Testament approved by the Catholic Church was printed at Douai in 1609–1610, and the Bible for English Catholics is known as the Douai Version.

Most English nonconformist books probably were printed at Middelburg, and the best-known printer of them was Richard Schilders. Originally from Hainaut, Schilders had taken refuge in England and had been admitted a brother of the Stationers' Company. In view of his real ability and limited opportunities, it is not surprising that he moved on to Middelburg and there became the official printer for the States of Zeeland. As has been said, there were congregations of Brownists and Puritans at Middelburg, and in addition the Merchant Adventurers maintained a chapel there. Schilders printed a number of books for Browne of the Brownists and for the successive chaplains to the Merchant Adventurers, Thomas Cartwright, Dudley Fenner, and others. At Dort there was a Puritan refugee press where several works were printed for Barrow and Greenwood. At Leyden, the Pilgrim Fathers had a press; at Amsterdam some English works were published, and here also the first English newspaper was issued. Although a considerable number of English books were printed in the Netherlands in the age of Elizabeth and James, only a beginning had been made, for later in the seventeenth century the printing of English books was a lucrative phase of Netherlands publishing.

Literary Relations. One evening in September, 1608, Thomas Coryate arrived at the town of Gorcum. "The sweetness of the

Plate 11. Sir Thomas Gresham's Royal Exchange in London. Engraved by Wenceslas Hollar, 1644.

situation," he wrote, "the elegancy of their buildings, the beauty of their streets, and all things whatsoever in this town, did wonderfully delight me, insomuch that as soon as I entered into one of the longer streets, methought I was suddenly arrived in the Thessalian Tempe or the Antiochian Daphne." Like a typical tourist, Coryate departed the next day, but he capitalized on his travels in the Netherlands, as did many another Englishman, by writing about the country in his travel book, *Coryate's Crudities, Hastily Gobbled up in Five Months' Travels* (1611). Other literary Englishmen who wrote about their travels in the Netherlands in this era include John Leland (1549), Sir Thomas Overbury, Sir Edwin Sandys, and Fynes Moryson. In the seventeenth century, after the period covered here, travelers who wrote of their experiences include John Evelyn, Samuel Pepys, and Owen Felltham. There were also many literary figures who, although they did not write travel books, lived and worked in the Netherlands and in some instances used their experience abroad in their writings. John Haywood lived, an exile, for many years in the South Netherlands. Nicholas Breton visited Antwerp, and Cyril Tourneur lived at Brielle, where his father was Lieutenant Governor. George Gascoigne and Thomas Churchyard served as soldiers in the Low Countries. Ben Jonson in his youth also served for a short time in the Netherlands, and it is possible that both Sir Walter Raleigh and George Chapman were soldiers there. The writer on economics Gerard Malynes was born at Antwerp, and Thomas Bodley, a powerful friend of literature and scholarship, spent much time in the Low Countries. Of these men, George Gascoigne and Thomas Churchyard used their Netherlands experience most extensively in their writings. In June, 1572, George Gascoigne arrived in Zeeland with a group of mercenaries to fight against Spain on the side of the Netherlands. He wrote of his experiences in that campaign in *The Fruits of War, Written upon This Theme, Dulce bellum inexpertis* ("Sweet is war to the inexperienced," a phrase taken from Erasmus) and also in *Gascoigne's Voyage into Holland.* Gascoigne was an eyewitness to the sack of Antwerp by the mutinous Spanish troops in 1576 and wrote an account of it, *The Spoil of Antwerp Faithfully Reported by a True Englishman* [1577?], one of the most graphic descriptions of a scene of horror in our language. One of his best-known works, *The Glass of Government; A Tragical Comedy* (1575), is apparently a translation of a morality which Gascoigne had procured in the Netherlands, and to which he perhaps added some adornments of his own. The debt of Churchyard to the Netherlands is even heavier than is that of Gascoigne. Those of his works which were the result of Netherlands experience include *A Lamentable and Pitiful Description of the Woeful Wars in Flanders* (1578), *A Pleasant Labyrinth Called Churchyard's Chance* (1579), *A Plain or Most True Report of a Dangerous Service for the Taking of Mechlin* (1580), and *The First Part of Churchyard's Chips* (1575).

The war in the Netherlands furnished material for a great number of writers in addition to Gascoigne and Churchyard, but few of their writings can be classed as literature. For example, Sir Roger Williams, John Waymouth, and Francis and Gervase Markham also wrote about the conflict. The tragic death of Oldenbarnevelt in 1619 gave occasion for a flood of books, but the theme, as might be expected, ran a short course. A number of pamphlet accounts appeared immediately after his death, giving some facts about his life, and within four months of his execution the King's company at Blackfriars staged *The Tragedy of Sir John of Oldenbarnevelt;* but this historical incident soon ceased to interest the public.

The idiosyncrasies of the Dutch character proved more durable and became the most popular Netherlandish theme for English authors. Happily for English writers, if they portrayed Dutchmen as stupid, crude characters, their audiences were delighted, and if they portrayed them as hard, shrewd, cunning men of business, that characterization seemed equally valid. In fact, to derogate the Dutch in any way was acceptable, as is evident from such popular phrases as "Dutch courage," "Dutch treat," "a Dutch bargain" (an agreement concluded when both parties were drunk), "a Dutch feast" (where the host is drunk before the guests), "a Dutch widow" (a strumpet), and "a

1. Gorleston

2. Enkhuizen

3. Over

4. Nymegen

5. Scole

6. Zwolle

7. Norwich

8. Franeker

Plate 12. A comparison of English and Dutch gables, from Cambridge Antiquarian Society *Proceedings,* XXXVII (1937). Reproduced by courtesy of the Society.

Dutch defense" (a treacherous betrayal). There is nothing particularly Dutch about the treacherous courtesan in John Marston's *The Dutch Courtesan,* but evidently to label her Dutch added something to the play's appeal.

The stupid Dutchman was a stock comic character. Such a Dutchman was Hans Beer-Pot in Belchier's play *Hans Beer-Pot* (1618), and such was Hans Van Belch in Thomas Dekker and John Webster's *Northward Ho!* (1607). In William Haughton's *Englishmen for My Money; or, A Pleasant Comedy Called, A Woman Will Have Her Will* (1616), the Dutchman Vandalle and two other foreigners share the humiliation of losing their sweethearts to three sturdy Englishmen. The Dutchman as a shrewd man of business is exhibited in the play *The Peddler's Prophecy,* which has been ascribed to Robert Wilson. In this play it is observed that:

> Our commodities away they do send,
> Rob and steal from Englishmen daily.

It also becomes apparent in the course of the play that the foreigners are responsible for native workmen starving, since the aliens take the available jobs; that they contaminate the English blood by marrying Englishwomen; and that, being "Anabaptists, Libertines, Epicureans, and Arians," they disturb the country with alien beliefs. The last charge is repeated in the play *New Custom,* where it is observed that:

> Since these Genevan doctors came so fast into this land,
> Since that time it was never merry with England.

George Wapull's play *The Tide Tarrieth No Man* gives the additional information that native Englishmen cannot find places to live because Netherlanders and Frenchmen take the houses.

> For among us now such is our country zeal
> That we love best with strangers to deal.
> To sell a lease dear, whosoever that will,
> At the French or Dutch church let him set up his bill,
> And he shall have chapmen, I warrant you, good store;
> Look what an Englishman bids, they will give him as much more.

The same theme appears in Robert Wilson's *The Three Ladies of London*. The Italian usurer Mercatore advises Lady Lucre how to get high rents for her tenements.

Madonna me tell ye vat you shall do,
Let dem to strangers dat are content
To dwell in a little room and to pay much rent.
For you know da Frenchmans and Flemings in dis country be many,
So dot they make shift to dwell ten houses in one very gladly
And be content a for pay fifty or threescore pound a year
For dat which da Englishman say twenty mark is too dear.

In the literature of the day, then, Dutchmen are stupid fellows, grasping fellows, a disruptive influence in religion, and disturbers of the social system. Such depiction may only reflect a human inclination to blame any aliens for whatever is wrong; and the Dutch, the most numerous of the aliens in England, received the blame.

The Netherlands cannot be said to have enriched English literature with new literary forms, but that region was instrumental in popularizing two forms already known, the emblem book and the *comedia sacra*. One of the more popular plays in the latter genre was *Acolastus* by Gnaphaeus, whose true name was Willem de Volder. The secret of the play's success is simple. The theme here is that of the Prodigal Son, but nearly all of the scenes in the play are concerned with the hero's riotous living and very little attention is given to the painful subject of repentance. *Acolastus* was the most popular Latin drama of the age, both in England and on the Continent. It was translated into English in 1540 by John Palsgrave and was acted at Cambridge in 1560 and 1561. John Lyly was still only a boy when the author, then a noted figure, visited England, yet so familiar was *Acolastus* even in Lyly's adult years that he chose names from the play for two of the main characters in his *Euphues*. In 1600, sixty years after the comedy had first been translated into English, two incidents occurred which showed that *Acolastus* was far from dead. In that year Samuel Nicholson, in an attempt to capitalize on the play's popularity, pub-

HANS
BEER-POT
HIS INVISIBLE
COMEDIE, OF
See me, and See me not.

ACTED
In the Low Countries, by an honeſt Company
of Health-Drinkers.

Omne tulit punctum qui miſcuit vtile dulci.

LONDON,
Imprinted by *Bernard Alſop*, and are to be ſolde at
his houſe by Saint *Annes* Church neere
Alderſgate, 1 6 1 8.

Plate 13. Dabridgcourt Belchier's popular *Hans Beer-Pot* (1618).

lished a book entitled *Acolastus His Afterwit*, and Jonson's play *Cynthia's Revels* had a character, "the little humanitian," named "Acolastus-Polypragmon-Asotus," by means of which Jonson poked fun at the *comedia sacra*.

A Dutchman, Jan van der Noot, was the author and compiler of what was probably the first emblem book in English. A translation of his "Theater of Voluptuous Worldlings" was issued in 1569–1570. The compiler took some verses from Petrarch, some from Du Bellay, and contributed some himself. In 1591 Edmund Spenser, among the poems of *Complaints*, reprinted as his own verses which had appeared in van der Noot's publication. The first Englishman to put together an emblem book was Geoffrey Whitney, who had been a student at Leyden and who published his *A Choice of Emblems and Other Devices* at Leyden in 1586. Janus Dousa, one of the original curators of the University, and Bonaventura Vulcanius, one of the early professors, both contributed verses to Whitney's book. Whitney took other verses from the famous emblem book of a Netherlander named Hadrianus Junius.

Language. The movement of soldiers, writers, and merchants between the two countries resulted in a far wider understanding of the Dutch language in England than exists today, and a number of Dutch words passed into English. The soldiers brought back from the Netherlands such words as *linstock*, *beleaguer*, *jerkin*, and possibly *knapsack*. Elizabethan vagabonds also picked up a number of Dutch words which possibly had also been brought back by soldiers or camp followers: a *pad* was a road, (Dutch *pad*); a *padder* was a robber (cf. footpad); *prad* meant a horse (Dutch *paard*). The commercial intercourse between these two seafaring peoples brought into our language a host of Dutch words: *ahoy, aloof, avast, caboose, hoist, hold* (of a ship), *hoy, hull, lash* (as in lashing spars together), *reef* (of a sail), *reef* (a rock), *reeve, sheer off, skipper, smack, splice, strand* (of a rope), *swab, yawl, boom, cruise, sloop, yacht*. In the travel accounts of Englishmen of the period,

THE
Dutch Courtezan.

AS

IT WAS PLAYD IN THE
Blacke-Friars, by the Children
of her Maiesties Reuels.

VVritten
BY IOHN MARSTON.

AT LONDON,
¶ Printed by T. P. for *Iohn Hodgets,*
and are to be sould at his shop in
Paules Church-yard. 1605.

Plate 14. John Marston's *The Dutch Courtesan* (1605).

the writers occasionally employ Dutch words as a matter of course, knowing that their readers will be familiar with them.

Learning and Scholarship. Throughout the Elizabethan age there was a close connection between the scholars of the two regions, and English students were frequently to be found at the new University of Leyden, which was founded in 1575. Among the Dutch scholars who visited England were Hadrianus Junius, Franciscus Junius, Jan van den Driessche (Johannes Drusius), and Constantijn Huygens. Of these, Constantijn Huygens is probably the best known. He was a scholar, a man of letters, and a diplomat. He first visited England in 1618 and revisited the country a number of times later. He met John Donne and subsequently translated into Dutch nineteen of Donne's poems and two poems by Ben Jonson. He wrote a brief poem on Hall's *Observations,* translated some of Quarles's "Emblems," and wrote a book of jests attributed to Archie Armstrong, King James's jester. When he visited Oxford, Huygens wrote a long poem on the University, praising particularly Christ Church and the Bodleian. In return, three Oxford scholars, Thomas Gall, Johannes Couperus, and Thomas Goffe, addressed poems to Huygens. Huygens considered Bacon's *Instauratio Magna* a most wonderful book, but when he met Bacon he disliked him. "What a monster of a man," he wrote, "than whom I remember seeing in the kingdom of Britain no one prouder, vainer, or more puffed up."

Hadrianus Junius, physician and typical sixteenth-century humanist, came to England about 1543 and was family physician to the Duke of Norfolk until the unfortunate Duke was beheaded. He was in England again in 1554 and wrote a poem to Philip and Mary, and in 1568 he paid a final visit to England. Drusius had been a student at Louvain. Coming to England with his Protestant father, he matriculated first at Cambridge, then at Oxford, and eventually became Regius Professor of Hebrew at Oxford. Franciscus Junius, although born at Heidelberg, was brought up at Leyden. Because he was a Remonstrant

Invidiam vincis studio, probitate labore.
Gratia nunc meritis reddita digna tuis.

Plate 15. Hadrianus Junius, from Jean Jacques Boissard, *Icones . . . virorum illustrium* (1597).

minister, he was dismissed from his office in 1619 and went to England in 1620, where he remained for most of the rest of his long life. One of the earliest Anglo-Saxon scholars, he published the biblical paraphrases of Caedmon and transcribed many Anglo-Saxon manuscripts. He also studied the cognate Teutonic languages and encouraged others to study them.

In this era, learning and scholarship were remarkably vigorous in the Netherlands, particularly at the University of Leyden, and not only England but other European countries were benefiting from that scholarship. As one result of this scholastic eminence, students flocked to Leyden from all over Europe. Students from England and Scotland at Leyden numbered 143 in the years 1571–1600, and 263 were enrolled in the period 1601–1625.

Farming and Gardening. The Netherlands influenced English country life in three ways: by stimulating an increase of sheep raising, introducing new flowers and vegetables, and providing the technical skill needed to drain the Fens.

England and the Netherlands were in an economic partnership in wool and cloth: the wool was raised in England, the cloth manufactured in both England and the Netherlands, and the product marketed in the latter country. Although domestic causes of enclosure and inflation, such as debasement of coinage and ordinary greed, were more potent, still the Netherlands-England partnership influenced both phenomena. The vast amounts of silver from the New World received in Spain affected the whole economy of Europe and caused a great and rapid increase in prices. So much Spanish silver was spent in the Netherlands that Spain remained poor and the Netherlands, that busy commercial center for Western Europe, became rich and prosperous. The Netherlands could thus pay much more for wool or cloth than before, and wool prices in England shot up. Cloth manufacturers were getting far more for their product and tenants were receiving far more for their wool and corn, but since land rents had been stable for centuries, landowners did not share in the new prosperity. Needless

Plate 16. Constantijn Huygens, as he appeared in the frontis-
piece to his *Momenta desultoria* (1655).

to say, the landlords were not content to be denied a share in the new wealth, and by increasing the amount of enclosed pastureage they began a change in the English countryside which was not completed until the eighteenth century.

The word "enclosure" might mean one of several operations. In the sixteenth century landlords began to overstock the common pasture with sheep and to persuade or force those who held land by copyhold to exchange that form of land title for simple tenancy at will, with the eventual purpose of converting the cultivated land into sheep pasturage. "Where there was once a great many householders and inhabitants," remarked Latimer, "there is now but a shepherd and his dog."

In order [exclaimed Thomas More] that one covetous and insatiable cormorant may compass about and enclose many thousand acres of ground together within one pale or hedge, the husbandmen be thrust out of their own, or by violent oppression they be put beside it, or by covin and fraud they be so wearied that they be compelled to sell all.

More goes on to lament that

by one means, therefore, or another, either by hook or crook, they must needs depart away, poor, silly, wretched souls, men, women, husbands, wives, fatherless children, widows, woeful mothers with their young babes, and their whole household, small in substance and much in number, as husbandry requireth many hands, . . . and when they have wandered about till the little they got by sale of their goods be spent, what can they then else do but steal and then justly, pardy, be hanged, or go about begging?

The amount of land enclosed was but a small fraction of the total arable land, but this fact has not a great deal of bearing on the significance of what was happening. In the first place, enclosures were most prevalent in East Anglia and the south coast regions, those areas most affected by the Netherlands market; and in the second place many men were aware that a trend had been started and that English country life was undergoing a permanent change, a change in which the Netherlands played not a dominant but still an important role.

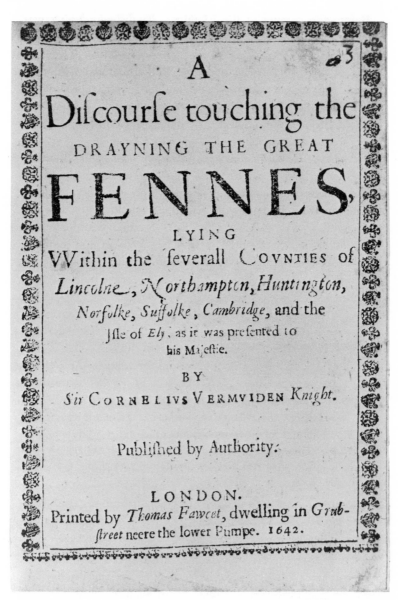

Plate 17. Sir Cornelius Vermuyden's treatise on the draining of the Fens.

Before the coming of the Flemings, English gardening was in a rudimentary state. Catherine of Aragon had her table supplied from the Low Countries, since vegetables for salads were not to be had in England. The Netherlanders by example gave a great stimulus to truck gardening. Cabbages, asparagus, artichokes, and water cress all became widely known and relished through the influence of the Low Country men, and the cultivation of flowers also owed much to them.

The other notable Netherlands influence was on the drainage of the Fens. One of the first of the Netherlanders interested in fen drainage was Humphrey Bradley, an engineer of high reputation from Brabant who had been employed on the improvement of Dover harbor. In 1593 Bradley wrote "A Discourse of Humphrey Bradley, a Brabanter, concerning the Fens in Norfolk." Other Low Country men were consulted about fen drainage, among them Guillaume Mostart, who undertook to drain the Fens of Coldham in Cambridgeshire, but large-scale fen drainage really begins with the interest taken in the problem by the Russell family, which possessed large acreage of fenlands in Cambridgeshire. William Russell, first Baron Russell of Thornhaugh, who had served for years in the Netherlands wars, brought over in 1590 from the Low Countries three experts in drainage, Jan Petersen, Jan Jacobson, and Waris Alart, to examine the Russell fenlands. Lord Russell applied to the Privy Council for permission both to drain the lands and to bring over Dutch families to settle on them. Although the project was not carried out, it had important results, for when Lord Russell died his son Francis formed a company to drain hundreds of thousands of acres of fenland and engaged Cornelius Vermuyden to undertake the work. This impressive engineering feat was carried out by Vermuyden after the end of the period covered here, but it had its beginnings in the age of Elizabeth.

By their connection with fen drainage and enclosures the Netherlands affected the English countryside, but individual Dutchmen also influenced English farms and gardens. Among these were Matthias de L'Obel, Rembert Dodoens, and the

Plate 18. A portrait of Anne of Denmark, after a painting from the studio of Paul van Somer. Reproduced courtesy of the National Portrait Gallery, London.

family of Tradescant. L'Obel was born at Lille in 1538 and practiced medicine at Antwerp and Delft before coming to England. Like other physicians of the time, he sought for cures among herbs and plants and so was a botanist as well as a man of medicine. He served as botanist to James I and for many years was in charge of the gardens of Lord Zouche at Hackney. The lobelia is named for him. Rembert Dodoens was born at Malines in 1517 and, although he did not live in England, he exerted great influence on English botany. He published in Dutch at Antwerp in 1554 a history and description of plants which owed much to Dioscorides. This book was translated into French and from French into English, the English translation also being published at Antwerp in 1578. Later Dodoens revised this work, and the revision, *Stirpium historiae pemptades* (1583), is one of the landmarks in herbal literature. John Gerard's *Herbal*, perhaps the best known of English herbals of the period, is founded entirely on Dodoens, and parts of Gerard are exact translations of Dodoens' work.

Probably the busiest gatherers of plants in England were the three generations of John Tradescants. The first John Tradescant came to England from the Low Countries in the reign of James I. His son was gardener to the first Lord Salisbury, to Lord Wotton, to the Duke of Buckingham, and to Charles I. His son, in turn, was also interested in botany, and all three generations of John Tradescants made voyages to various parts of the world to study plants. Incidentally they picked up many curious artifacts, which were exhibited in a museum known as Tradescant's Ark. The museum was bequeathed to Elias Ashmole, who in turn bequeathed it to the University of Oxford.

This booklet began with the statement that the English of Elizabeth's reign had something to learn from the Netherlands in almost every line of endeavor. The Low Country provinces were the banking, manufacturing, and trading center for Western Europe and possessed the wealth necessary to support a vigorous community of artists, craftsmen, scholars, and writers. While the Netherlands was at the center of civilization, England was still on the periphery; hence it is not surprising that Eng-

land learned from the Low Countries. The position of Britain
vis-à-vis the Netherlands was not much different from that of
other countries of Europe. Netherlands musicians influenced
Italian music; Low Country painters had great success in Spain;
Dutchmen secured a place in French commercial life; and
Netherlands scholarship attracted students from many countries.

The Netherlands and Belgium today do not exert great political power in the world, but in the age of Elizabeth I the people of the Low Countries influenced all Europe in many ways
and in a measure far greater than the size and political power
of the area would indicate. The age of Elizabeth I in England
can be better understood if one remembers that England
turned to the Low Countries, not only for many of the good
things of life, but for instruction in the arts and skills that
advanced English civilization.

SUGGESTED READING

There are three works which deal specifically with the subject of this booklet. They are William Cunningham, *Alien Immigrants to England* (London, 1897), Johan F. Bense, *Anglo-Dutch Relations from the Earliest Times to the Death of William the Third* (The Hague, 1925), and an article by John J. Murray, "The Cultural Impact of the Flemish Low Countries on Sixteenth- and Seventeenth-Century England," *American Historical Review*, LXII (1957), 837–854. The facts of Netherlands-English relations before the age of Elizabeth can be found in general histories of England and the Low Countries and to a large extent in economic histories also. Particularly useful are Petrus J. Blok, *History of the People of the Netherlands* (5 vols., New York, 1898–1912); Henri Pirenne, *Economic and Social History of Medieval Europe* (London, 1936); Ephraim Lipson, *The Economic History of England* (3 vols., London, 1915–1931); William Cunningham, *The Growth of English Industry and Commerce* (3 vols., Cambridge, 1927–1938); and Bernard H. M. Vlekke, *Evolution of the Dutch Nation* (New York, 1945).

The literature on English-Netherlandish trade is remarkably voluminous. Particularly interesting, although not confined to this subject, is the collection of documents by Richard H. Tawney and Eileen Power, *Tudor Economic Documents* (3 vols., London, 1951). Two works already mentioned, that by Ephraim Lipson and Cunningham's three volumes on industry and commerce, are also immensely useful. The Merchant Adventurers were treated by George Unwin in "The Merchant Adventurers Company in the Reign of Elizabeth," which appeared in *Economic History Review*, I (1927), 36–54, and was republished in George Unwin, *Studies in Economic History, the Collected Papers of George Unwin* (London, 1927; 1958). Conyers Read also wrote on English trade in this period in his "English Foreign Trade under Elizabeth," *English Historical Review*, XXLX (1914), 515–524. Much interesting information on

Scottish trade will be found in John Davidson, *The Scottish Staple at Veere* (London, 1909).

The political relations of the two countries have also attracted a great number of writers, and indeed this phase is so important that most general histories have a chapter or section devoted to it. J. B. Black, *The Reign of Elizabeth* (Oxford, 1936; 1959) has an excellent discussion of this subject.

In the field of religion a fascinating book is John Tulloch, *Rational Theology and Christian Philosophy in England in the Seventeenth Century* (2 vols., Edinburgh, 1874). The same author also wrote *English Puritanism and Its Leaders* (Edinburgh and London, 1861). The Puritans are the subject of a voluminous literature. Particularly useful are Douglas Campbell, *The Puritan in England, Holland, and America* (New York and London, 1892; 4th ed., rev., 1902); Henry M. and Morton Dexter, *The England and Holland of the Pilgrims* (Boston, 1906); and Andrew F. S. Pearson, *Thomas Cartwright and Elizabethan Puritanism, 1535–1603* (Cambridge, 1925). A most interesting work on Arminianism is Archibald H. W. Harrison, *Arminianism* (London, 1937). The same author wrote *The Beginnings of Arminianism to the Synod of Dort* (London, 1926). An older work is George L. Curtis, *Arminianism in History* (Cincinnati, 1894). Writings on the Familists are rare in English, but there is a useful article on the sect in the *Schaff Herzog Encyclopedia*. The history of the English Catholics is told in John H. Pollen, *The English Catholics in the Reign of Queen Elizabeth* (London, 1920), and much information will also be found in Walter H. Frere, *The English Church in the Reigns of Elizabeth and James I* (London, 1904). The history of the Dutch Reformed Church in London is given by Johannes Lindeboom, *Austin Friars: History of the Dutch Reformed Church in London, 1559–1950,* trans., D. de Jongh (The Hague, 1950), and in William J. C. Moens, *The Marriage, Baptismal, and Burial Registers, 1571–1874, and Monumental Inscriptions of the Dutch Reformed Church, Austin Friars, London. With a Short Account of the Strangers and Their Churches* (Lymington, 1884).

A good impression of the importance of Netherlandish painters in Elizabethan times can be gotten from the illustrated catalogue of the Burlington Fine Arts Club, *Catalogue of an Exhibition of Late Elizabethan Art* (London, 1926). English painting is treated at great length in C. H. Collins Baker, *British Painting* (London, 1933). A very useful article on the Netherlanders in England is Lionel H. Cust, "Notes on Foreign Artists of the Reformed Religion in England from about 1560 to 1660," Huguenot Society, *Proceedings*, VII (1903), 45–82.

Material on engravers from the Netherlands can be found in A. M. Hind, *Engraving in England in the Sixteenth and Seventeenth Centuries. Part I. The Tudor Period* (Cambridge, 1952). An interesting article on the sculpture of the period is K. A. Esdaile, "The Inter-Action of English and Low Country Sculpture in the Sixteenth Century," *Journal of the Warburg and Courtauld Institutes*, VI (1943), 80–88.

For architecture, there is an extremely well-written and fascinating book, which is in fact useful for all the arts, James Lees-Milne, *Tudor Renaissance* (London and New York, 1951). The influence of Dutch domestic architecture in England is graphically presented in C. L. Cudworth, "Dutch Influence in East Anglian Architecture," Cambridge Antiquarian Society, *Proceedings*, XXXVII (1937), 24–42. Other useful books on architecture are John A. Gotch, *Architecture of the Renaissance in England* (2 vols., London, 1891–1894), and the same author's *Early Renaissance Architecture in England* (London, 1914). Reginald T. Blomfield, *A History of Renaissance Architecture in England, 1500–1800* (2 vols. London, 1897), is also useful.

There are a number of excellent books on English glassware and glassmaking, among them Daisy Wilmer, *Early English Glass of the Sixteenth, Seventeenth, and Eighteenth Centuries* (London, 1909), William A. Thorpe, *English Glass* (London, 1935), and Francis Buckley, *A History of Old English Glass* (London, 1925). A particularly valuable article is E. W. Hulme, "English Glassmaking in the Sixteenth and Seventeenth Centuries," *Antiquary*, XXX (1894), 210–214, 259–263. The general work on tapestry chiefly used in preparing this booklet is William G. Thomson, *A History of Tapestry* (London, 1930).

The influence of Netherlandish music is treated in such general books as Paul Henry Lang, *Music in Western Civilization* (New York, 1941). A more detailed discussion is the same author's "The So-called Netherlands School," *Musical Quarterly*, XXV (1939), 48–59. Madrigals are fully discussed in Edmund H. Fellowes, *English Madrigal Composers* (Oxford, 1921) and Renaissance music generally in Bruce Pattison, *Music and Poetry of the Renaissance* (London, 1948) and in Alec Harman, *Late Renaissance and Baroque Music* (London, 1959).

For Netherlands printers in England and English printers in the Netherlands see Ernest J. Worman, *Alien Members of the Book-Trade during the Tudor Period* (London, 1906); *Records of the Court of the Stationers' Company, 1576–1602* (2 vols., London, 1930–1957); Alfred Pollard, "English Books Printed Abroad," Bibliographical Society, *Transactions*, III (1895–1896), 195–209; and J. Dover Wilson, "Richard Schilders and the English Puritans," Bibliographical Society, *Transactions*, XI (1909–1911), 65–134.

A very useful treatment of literary influences is contained in a series of articles with various titles by Abraham Bronson Feldman in *Notes and Queries* for the years 1951–1952. The same author wrote "Gnaphaeus in England," *Modern Language Notes*, LXVII (1952), 325–328. An older work, really not very enlightening but always mentioned, is Jan David de Vries, *Holland's Influence on English Language and Literature* (Chicago, 1916). Also useful for this section are the standard editions of the works of English authors. Walter W. Skeat, *Principles of English Etymology* (Oxford, 1891) discusses Dutch words in the English language. Netherlandish literary influences and Netherlands scholarship are illuminated by Alfred G. H. Bachrach, *Sir Constantine Huygens and Britain: 1596–1687* (Leyden, 1962), and Rosalie Colie, *'Some thankfulnesse to Constantine': A Study of English Influence upon the Early Works of Constantijn Huygens* (The Hague, 1956).

The Netherlandish influence in gardening is discussed in Alicia Amherst (Mrs. Evelyn Cecil), *A History of Gardening in England* (London, 1910), and Reginald T. Blomfield, *The Formal Garden in England* (London, 1901). Lawrence E. Harris gives an excellent account of fen drainage in *Vermuyden and the Fens* (London, 1953) and Richard H. Tawney a most interesting account of land enclosure in *The Agrarian Problem in the Sixteenth Century* (London, 1912).